Zero Capital Self-Publishing Secrets (How To Publish EBooks & Paperbacks On Over 20 Publishing Companies Without A Dime)

DAVID KPRAKE.

Copyright © 2020 David Kprake.

AMAZON EDITION 2020

UPDATED VERSION 2023

All rights reserved. No part of this publication may be reproduced, stored in a retrieval system, or transmitted in any form or by any means, electronic, mechanical, photocopying or otherwise, without the prior permission of the copyright owner.

ISBN:9798647780379

DEDICATION

This book is dedicated to Dr. Paul Oronana Edugbo.

CONTENTS

Acknowledgments	i
Introduction	1
Writing your book	4
Creating your book cover	5
Editing your book	6
Book formatting	8
Publishing an EBook on many platforms	15
Publishing the paperback	34
Marketing your book	38
Other Platforms To Publish Your Books Or Ebooks.	40
About David Kprake	41

ACKNOWLEDGMENTS

Special thanks to all our contributors.

Illustrations: Cover: David Kprake

Editors: Newskylight.

Computer Works: Newskylight Press

ZERO CAPITAL SELF PUBLISHING SECRETS.

BOOKS BY DAVID KPRAKE

NOW OUT!
CRIME SERIES.

INTRODUCTION

Welcome to the digital-age where self-publishing has replaced the traditional publishing industry. Today, with little or no capital, you can self-publish a book which in the past you must pay to get your book published. It was also more expensive to distribute your books from bookshop to bookshop. But with these digital platforms, with a click, your they will be available all-over-the-world. My books right now are being read in Canada, the US, the UK, Germany, China, France, India, Australia, Japan, etc.

In this book: Zero capital self-publishing secrets. (How to publish eBooks and paperback on over 20 self-publishing companies) we intend to reveal secrets that will enable you to publish your book all over the world without spending any money. In this book, we also intended to give you links to these websites. But we are at the mercy of the retailers who may not allow the links. We will be glad to offer support via our email:

kdtechglobal@gmail.com.

The good news is that self-publishing in these platforms is FREE! But if you request our service to help to publish your books on these platforms, you have to pay. With this training, you can do it yourself and not spend even a dime.

You're required to create the following accounts before registering with any of the platforms:

ZERO CAPITAL SELF PUBLISHING SECRETS.

1. Email account (Gmail or yahoo mail, e.g. Kdtechglobal@gmail.com)

2. Foreign bank account: sign-up with any one of them using your email to receive your royalties from these sites where you uploaded your books because they won't send money into your account.

1. Payoneer- use this code to open your Payoneer account and get a $25 bonus

   https://bit.ly/2U7dM6G

2. Transferwise- create a Transferwise account using your email on this code. https://transferwise.com/invite/u/e7b9604

3. Paypal- Create a Paypal account using your email to sign up.

https://www.paypal.com/ls/webapps/mpp/merchant

Publishing Partners:

To save you the rigours of registering with all the 20 sites, visit these partners to get your job done. They will assist you to distribute your books in all the publishing sites. They are:

1. Smashwords 2. Draft2digital 3. Publishdrive.

One important reason to use these publishing partners is that they can publish and distribute your books on platforms that do not support authors from your country (e.g. Nigeria) platforms as – Google Play, Barnes & Noble, etc.

Another important reason to use these publishing partners is that they will take your book and distribute it to a list of publishing retailers, control the analytics, collect royalties, and pay you in one lump sum.

Publishdrive partners include:

Amazon, Apple, Kobo, Barnes and Noble, Scribd, 24symbols, Google Play, Overdrive, Rakuten Kobo, and Kobo plus, and as they continue to add more partners.

Draft2digital partners include:

Amazon, IBooks, Inktera, Baker & Taylor, Biblioteca, Playster, Mobile phone Apps, Cloud Library, Odilo, 24-symbols, Scribd, Barnes and Noble, Tolino, Kobo, Overdrive, Google Play, and Apple, and as they continue to add more partners.

Smashwords partners include:

Apple, Kobo, Tolino, Overdrive, Scribd, Barnes and Noble, Cloud Library, Odilo, Gardners, Askew & holts, Brown books for students, Califa, Livraria Cultura, and as they continue to add more partners.

WRITING YOUR BOOK.

To write a book used to be through inspiration. You could write from experience or write about your experiences. But today, you can write a book as soon as you follow some processes. You research the topic that you want to write. Be it on health and fitness or how to make money online and write your book. So, get a book title as the starting point. Then start to write. You can decide to hire a freelancer on 'Fiverr' or 'Upwork' to write on your chosen topic or title at a negotiated price. Next, get your book edited. Get a friend in that field who is an English graduate to help you. Also download apps like Grammarly, to correct your spellings and tenses.

When you use a freelancer to write the book, you should check for plagiarism by checking your book at 'Copyscape'.

CREATING YOUR BOOK COVER.

Creating The Cover

We have bestselling authors who could sell a book with only their names printed on the cover. But some of us must design beautiful covers and good titles to enable us to attract sales.

You can design one for yourself or pay a professional to do it.

Design cover In producing a cover, you will need your camera to capture good live photos or download free ones from Unsplash, Pixaby, and Depositphotos. You are to read and follow their terms of use.

You will then go further to design the book cover in CorelDraw and Photoshop.

Amazon can also allow you to use their free photos or images. But you can only use it to publish on their platform.

Take note, if you publish a paperback, you must use the correct book size to match your book cover size.

When you still cannot design a good book cover, you should hire a freelancer. Try Fiverr, Canva or Upwork.

EDITING YOUR BOOK.

You must upload a well written, edited and proofread book to the publishing platform. To correct your grammar, I recommend downloading 'Grammarly' at www.grammarly.com

Need Help? If you don't have the time, patience or skills to properly format your book to Standard requirements, consider hiring us at NEWSKYLIGHT at a reasonable fee.

Contact us: kdtechglobal@gmail.com

Editing your manuscript is very essential. It is advisable to self-edit before you send it to an editor. Every author indeed needs an editor. You will still need an editor to ensure that your manuscript is as polished as possible. Some clues to self-editing include:

1. Turn on your computer's spell-check function and run a spell-check. After which you use your "Grammarly" to further edit your book.

2. Remove or replace your "crutch words"- these are those words that you keep on using or keep on falling back on.

3. Remove all double spaces at the end of sentences.

4. Set your book aside for at least one week without reading or working on it. When you return to read the book, it becomes a fresh work and you can discover more errors to correct.

Useful Tips.

- Research on the topic or idea that you are writing on. Is it on health and fitness? How to make money online etc.

- Keywords – For your book to be discoverable you need to search the words that people will search for online.

- Book Description-This is the synopsis of your book that people will see and read first. If it is well written, it will lead to the sale of the book.

- Plagiarism. To check whether your work is a product of another person's work when you consulted a freelancer to write the book. Go to www.copyscape.com to find out.

   Copyscape is a free plagiarism checker. The software lets you detect duplicate content and check if your text is original.

   - Does your book have adult contents? This is to find out if your book is for adult readership only. You must be honest with your assertions to prevent rejection or sanction.

BOOK FORMATTING

Book formatting to meet industry standard begin when you are about to start typing your work. You must first adjust your settings in Microsoft word.

1. If you have images or pictures to add to your book, never you copy and paste. You must insert your images. Go to INSERT menu and click on picture which will launch you to your files. Select your jpg file and insert into your document. Then click the centre(ctrl+e)

2. Go to page layout, paragraph, then select "first line" and set your indent at standard publishing 0.5" (but in epub, set it at 0.3")

3. Uncheck the Autocorrect button. In Autocorrect English (US), uncheck all the check marks then click ok.

4. Set up your spacing between paragraphs at page layout tab. Reset the "After" option to 10 point (But in epub 0)

5. To pass the auto-vetting stage, you must not add "link" of any other retailer into your book. You must not have link of Amazon site or even mention them in your book when you're uploading to Smashwords site.

Creating Your Table Of Content.

There are differences between print book formatting

and eBook formatting.

With print books you use page numbers to navigate. While with eBooks you use hyperlinks to navigate. This is because eBooks are not supposed to have page numbers. If you don't get this right, you will not be able to pass the auto vetting stage for your Epub conversion at Smashwords.

A Table of Contents makes it easy for your readers to view the chapters of your book.

Type your table of contents at the start of your book, immediately following your title and copyright pages, and preceding the start of your Chapter One.

As you type, make sure your text is in the Normal paragraph style or a custom style. You're advised not to create your Table of Content in Heading style.

Go to the body of the book and highlight say Chapter one then click insert >bookmark. A bookmark box will appear. Under the Bookmark Name type C1 as chapter one (it must be one word not two words e.g. c1 not chapter 1. No space) and click "Add". Then go to the Table of content and highlight chapter one then click Hyperlink. A box will appear. At the left hand side, there is "place in the document" click it. Under "select a place in this document" click C1 then ok. Your chapter one will turn blue. It is OK.

Repeat the same process with chapter two, three etc.

Test your work by clicking on each linked item in your Table of Content to see if it goes to the proper destination.

Remove Hidden Bookmarks.

When you've finished testing the workability of your TOC, move to this next step. Ms Word usually introduces 'Hidden bookmarks' into your document and these hidden bookmarks can corrupt your TOC. Check for these hidden bookmarks and delete them. Click Insert: Bookmark, then click and unclick the checkbox by "Hidden Bookmarks." Hidden bookmarks start with an underline or underscore "_Hlt40386292" Click the name of the hidden bookmark then click the delete button at the right side. They may be so many. Delete them one by one.

How To Attract Your Customers' Patronage.

Category

To find the best categories for your book, search for categories on Amazon. E.g. kindle stores. Search for books like yours and see the categories assigned to these books. Also, search the books detail page at "Look for similar items by category". There you will find similar categories to use for your book.

Customer Reviews

The best way to find out what customers want is to read customer reviews from similar books like yours. You can find out from the review why they bought that book, it indicates to you if the book met their expectations. Take note of phrases or quotes to use in your book description. You are to look for the "Top customer reviews". This will guide you in knowing what your customers' expectations are. Thus, you can write to their taste which will in turn amount to your book sales.

Book Description

You must invest ample time in your book description because its main aim is to get sales. So, tailor it to your target audience. Let it show them the specific benefits they will derive from reading your book. Tell them how your book will solve their problems. Check the description from similar books. Also, check related books customers have bought under the "customers who bought this item also bought" column. This you will find under the book description section in Amazon. This will tell you your customers' expectation of what your book should address.

Formatting Your Book Description.

Amazon has an option for formatting your book description into an HTML format. The plain text format for Amazon's book description is not very attractive. It is looking clumsy. With the HTML style, you can make your text bold. You can also add italics, bullets, underlines, paragraphs, and increase the font size to make it attractive and readable.

To format your book description into the HTML format, use the 'Kindlepreneur Amazon Book description generator,' then you are good to go.

https://kindlepreneur.com/amazon-book-description-generator/#

Keywords

Choosing the right keywords increases the chances of your book's visibility on publishing platforms.

Keywords promote your book's online visibility. Don't repeat keywords. What forms your general keywords are: book title, sub-title, book description, and your seven keywords.

To get to your target audience, keywords play important role. So, use these tools.

- Amazon Autosuggestions.

Amazon Autosuggestions is another great tool to use for finding keywords. When you type any word into Amazon search bar, its search engine will then suggest words that other customers are using to search for that same product and thus suggest keywords for you to use.

- Google Autosuggestions

As Amazon autosuggestion provides keyword suggestions when you type in your keyword or phrase, so is Google autosuggestion.

- Keywordtool.io provides keyword suggestions for YouTube, Amazon, Bing, and Google. You can also search by location. You can search for what keywords people are searching for in the US, London, Nigeria etc.

- Seo chat keywords suggest tool

Provides autosuggestions for Amazon, Google, Bing, and YouTube.

-keyword.io- this tool will help you with a comprehensive list of relevant keyword suggestions to create and improve your message and connect with your audience better. It helps you to find the actual phrases people are using to find information, products and services. You only have to create a free account enabling you to download the generated list. It is very easy to open the account.

-Jaaxy – Jaaxy can "dig" as deep as you want and save you hours per week on your research activities, giving you more time to work on other aspects of your business. Sign up and get 30 searches free.

-SEMrush- All-purpose approach to keyword research. Get a free trial.

-KWFinder covers both traditional and competitor keyword research to help you find long-tail keywords with low SEO difficulty. Try it for free!

- Soovle is a customizable engine that unites the suggestion services from all the major providers in one place: Google, Bing, Amazon, Answers.com, Yahoo, Wikipedia, YouTube. I found the tool to be a major help for search and content creation inspiration.

PUBLISHING AN EBOOK ON MANY PLATFORMS.

How To Publish On Amazon.

Amazon is the biggest free online marketplace in the entire world. The number one self-publishing company globally trailed by Apple books as number two.

Amazon has changed the publishing world from where it was. The traditional publishing firms frustrated so many authors in time past.

You are now in a position to write and publish your work and meet the success authors often dream of.

Simple procedure:
- Create your account
- Fill your tax information details
- Enter your book details
- Upload your manuscript/cover files
- Set your price
- Publish.

To Self Publish on Amazon. Firstly, use their authors/publishers website https://www.kdp.amazon.com

ZERO CAPITAL SELF PUBLISHING SECRETS.

Secondly, create an account with them by using your email address and a password. Please don't use any fake address or email address.
Kindle Direct Publishing.

- Set up your account (sign up)
- Write your book description
- Build your Amazon detail page
- Introduction to book design
- Format your eBook manuscript
- Format your paperback manuscript
- Design your cover
- Upload your book
- EBook rights & pricing
- Paperback right & pricing

NOW BEGIN
Sign up
Create account
Your name
Email
Password
Re enter password
After you have created your kdp account, enter and click Bookshelf. You will see *BOOK CONTENT *BOOK COVER *DESCRIPTION, KEYWORDS AND CATEGORIES. *ISBN.

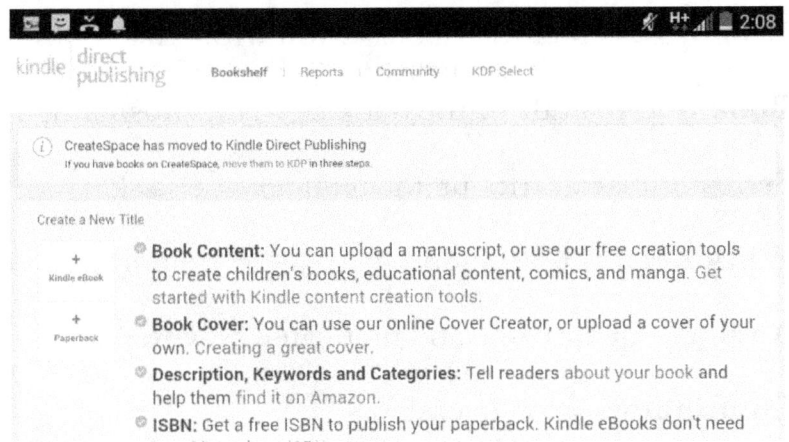

Before you start to upload your books, as a beginner, please click each and study all. Starting with BOOK CONTENT proceed to BOOK COVER then DESCRIPTION, KEYWORDS AND CATEGORIES, finally ISBN.

When you have acquainted yourself with all the processes you can then start to publish your book.

Now start by clicking 'create a new title'.

Under 'create a new title you have +kindle eBook and +paperback. When creating a paperback, click '+ paperback'.

When creating an eBook, click '+kindle eBook'.

This will launch you into filling the following:

Kindle EBook Details.

Language —enter the language you wrote the book.

Book title-the title of the book e.g. Tiny Mosquitoes.

Series-if it is in series fill the number or else skip.

Edition-if it is first edition then say 1st Edition.

Author-your surname and first name as writer.

Contributors - you may skip.

Description - (see inside this manual for details)

Publishing rights - That you have the copyright.

Keywords (7) - (see inside this manual for details)

Categories (2)-use the dropdown menu and select two categories that your book belongs.

Age & grade - those the book is written for.

Pre order - (skip)

Save & continue - enter or click. The next page will appear.

ZERO CAPITAL SELF PUBLISHING SECRETS.

Sample from one of my books, *Little David and the Seven Giants by David Kprake.*

Manuscript (yes)

Upload eBook manuscript

As a beginner, download the Kindle Create:

https://www.amazon.com/Kindle-Create/b?ie=UTF8&node=18292298011

And the kindle Previewer.

If you want to see how your eBook will look before you publish it, use Kindle Previewer.

https://kdp.amazon.com/en_US/help/topic/G202131170

& Kindle eBook cover: two options;

-use their cover creator tool or

-a cover you already designed

Launch previewer

ISBN – eBooks are not required to have ISBN.

Publish

Save and continue

ZERO CAPITAL SELF PUBLISHING SECRETS.

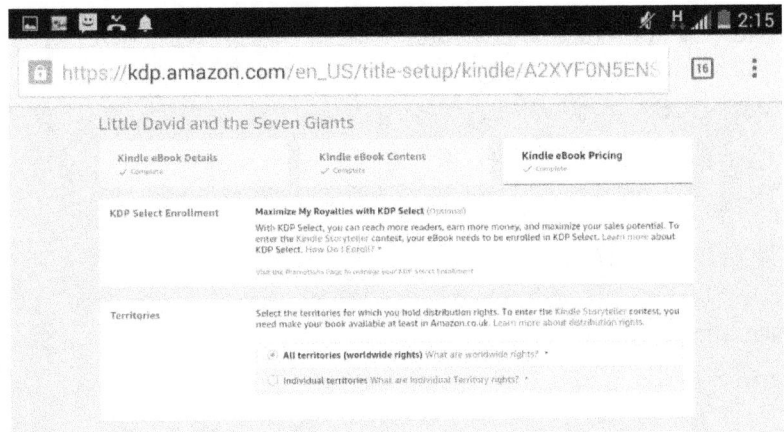

KDP Select Enrollment (Skip so that you can publish on other platforms)

Territories –enter all territories for your book to be sold worldwide.

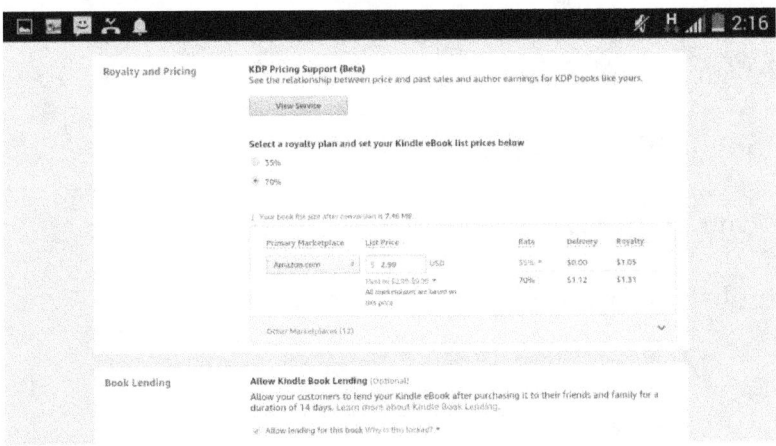

Royalty & pricing

Select a royalty plan

35% or 70%

Under you will see primary market place eg Amazon.com

List price e.g. $1.99

Rate   35%

Delivery   0.00

Royalty $0.70

70%

List price e.g. $2.99

Rate   70%

Delivery $1.04

Royalty $1.36

Book lending (SKIP)

Terms & Conditions (read)

Publish your kindle eBook

ZERO CAPITAL SELF PUBLISHING SECRETS.

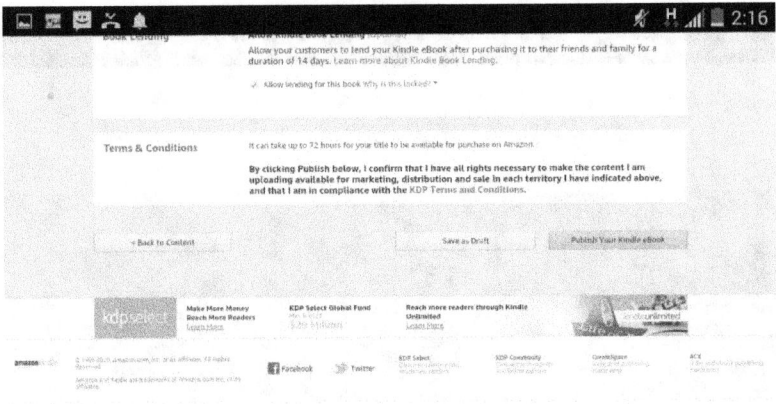

ZERO CAPITAL SELF PUBLISHING SECRETS.

Congratulations!

Your kindle eBook has been submitted.

LITTLE DAVID AND THE SEVEN GIANTS

BY DAVID KPRAKE

It can take up to 72 hours for your title to be available for purchase on Amazon

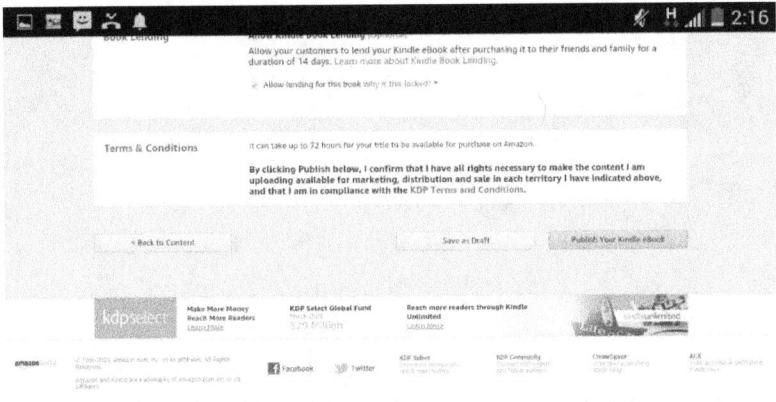

Next you can begin to monitor your sales.

Your sales dashboard will be found under REPORTS.

Click "report" and monitor your sales.

You can then proceed to publish your paper back. This aspect is more technical.

ZERO CAPITAL SELF PUBLISHING SECRETS.

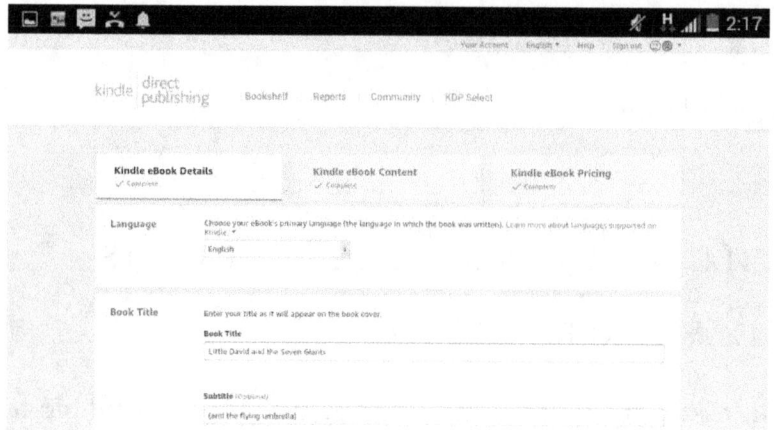

How To Publish On Draft2digital. {UPDATE: Smashwords is now part of Draft2digital. As of Feb 8, 2022 Draft2digital announced that they are acquiring Smashwords.

When you sign up with Draft2Digital, furnish them with the following information: Title, Description, Sales categories, and Keywords. Or you can submit your manuscript soft copy and they will do the technical parts. What you need to do is to mark your chapter breaks with something distinctive, and be consistent. Make it cantered and bold, or larger font, or use a Heading style. Do something to set apart your chapter titles, and they will take care of the rest.

How you receive your payment from draft2Digital

1. Check (register your contact with them)

2. PayPal (your email address that you used to open PayPal account)

3. Direct deposit (selected countries)

4. Payoneer (after you've created an account with them)

Draft2Digital will distribute your book to their dedicated partners which include:

Amazon, IBooks, Inktera, Baker & Taylor, Biblioteca, Playster, Mobile phone Apps, Cloud Library, Odilo, 24-symbols, Scribd, Barnes and Noble, Tolino, Kobo, Overdrive, Google Play, and Apple, and as they continue to add more partners.

Log in and register with draft2digital using my referral link. https://www.draft2digital.com/r/RkG9NR

How To Publish On Publishdrive.

PublishDrive is another self-publishing company.

They offer a range of services to help self-published authors and independent publishers.

They distribute your books to a global market. One special feature of PublishDrive is their free EBook converter. They can convert your manuscript from DOCX to EPUB and MOBI. Another special feature of PublishDrive is that you're allowed to Keep 100% of your royalties.

Publishdrive distributes EBooks to over 400 online stores and 240,000 digital libraries globally.

They also reach global markets like Google Play and China.

The partners include Amazon, Apple Books, Barnes & Noble, Rakuten Kobo, OverDrive, Bibliotheca, Scribd, 24Symbols, and Hoopla.

You can use my referral link by registering with your

email on:

https://admin.publishdrive.com/registration/aff/davidkprake

2023 UPDATE:

Publishdrive introduced a **PublishDrive's subscription model in 2019.**

'We introduced a monthly/annual subscription model back in 2019 where no matter how much you sell, you pay only the monthly fee of the plan of your choice and keep all of your royalties — all of your sales revenue. This way, authors can anticipate the cost of their distribution and also save way more time for writing or building their author brand.'

How To Publish On Smashword.

Firstly, I sincerely recommend that you download their free instructional EBook titled, Smashwords-Style-Guide. Study it religiously and then you are good to go. It will save you so much stress. This is the link for the free guide book. https://www.smashwords.com/books/view/52

To publish with Smashwords, sign up for a free account at Smashwords.com. After this, follow the instructions that comes up in your email.

Once you publish your book at Smashwords, they will

review it. If it meets the required standard, your book transmits to the retailers and libraries.

Different eBook File Types.

You have two options available in submitting your book to Smashwords.

1. You can upload your own designed Epub file. So far it is professionally done to standard.

2. You can upload a Microsoft Word document of the manuscript.

As soon as you upload a Word document to Smashwords, they automatically convert it into different file types which make your book accessible and readable to users of any e-reading device. These devices are the iPad, iPhone, Kindle, Nook, Kobo Reader, personal computers, and any smart phone.

EPUB - This is the standard format for eBooks. This is the format that is required by retailers like Apple, Barnes & Noble, Kobo, Oyster, Scribd, and others.

Mobipocket (Kindle) – Mobipocket(MOBI) This is popular with Amazon. It is a requirement for distribution to Amazon. Your book can now be read on the Amazon Kindle and many other e-reading devices.

HTML SmashReader – This is Smashwords' online reader that allows one to read from their store.

PDF - Portable Document Format is a file format that is more popular used by most devices and the personal computers.

Plain Text - Plain text is the most widely supported file format. It works on nearly all readers and devices. It lacks formatting, but will work anywhere so far your manuscript should not contain images or fancy formatting.

Palm Doc (PDB) - PalmDoc is a format used on Palm Pilot devices.

LRF - This is the former format for the Sony Reader. Sony later moved to the EPUB format.

RTF - Rich Text Format is a cross-platform document format supported by many word processors and devices.

MARKETING INFORMATION.

Congratulations! For you to get to this stage there is every possibility that Dollars will soon begin to roll into your pocket.

The next thing to do is to promote your work with every available tool at Smashwords.

Please download their marketing guide.

The Smashwords Book Marketing Guide at http://www.smashwords.com/books/view/305

Your Book Global Outreach.

The fastest and simplest way to reach the world with your book is to get it published at Smashwords.

Smashwords is the world's largest distributor of eBooks from self-published authors.

When you upload your manuscript in Microsoft word to Smashwords, they will take care of everything else.

They will produce the files and data necessary to support the unique requirements of each retailer and deliver everything to them per their requirements.

You'll be able to manage and track your eBook distribution through your Smashwords Dashboard as simple as A.B.C.

The Smashwords distribution network includes major eBook stores and libraries, including Apple iBooks, Barnes & Noble, Kobo, Flipkart, Oyster, Scribd, and over 30,000 public libraries around the world such as OverDrive, Bibliotheca CloudLibrary, Gardners, and Odilo.

If you want to change the price, or upload a new version of your book, or update your cover image or book description, you do it once from your Dashboard and then they will send the update out to all their retailers. You can update your book as often as you like. This also is a major time-saver for authors.

Another very important feature is access to powerful sales, marketing and merchandising tools.

These are available to Smashwords authors and publishers.

I recommend their podcast. Please take advantage of these free tools. Here is the link.
https://www.smashwords.com/podcast

To reach the Premium Catalog distribution stage, your book must meet a certain standard.

PUBLISHING THE PAPERBACK.

To publish your book in paperback, they have a very simple process.

www.kdp.amazon.com

When you sign in, on the dashboard you will see "publish in paperback or kindle".

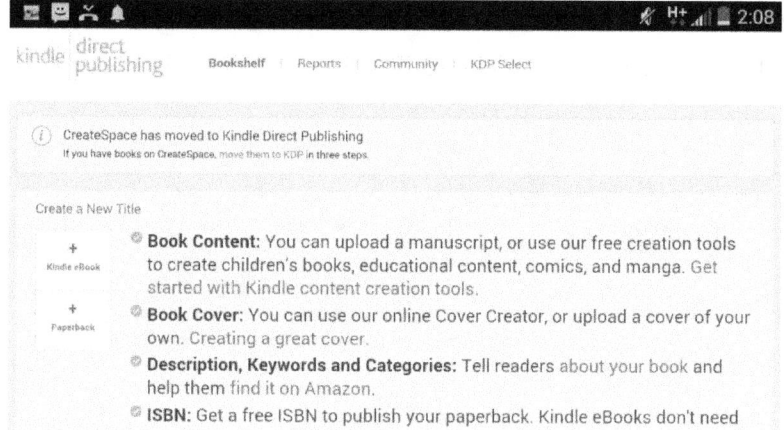

Enter under create a new title + paperback and continue.

ZERO CAPITAL SELF PUBLISHING SECRETS.

Where you don't understand the term used, there is a dropdown menu you click to explain the terms used in the form you're filling.

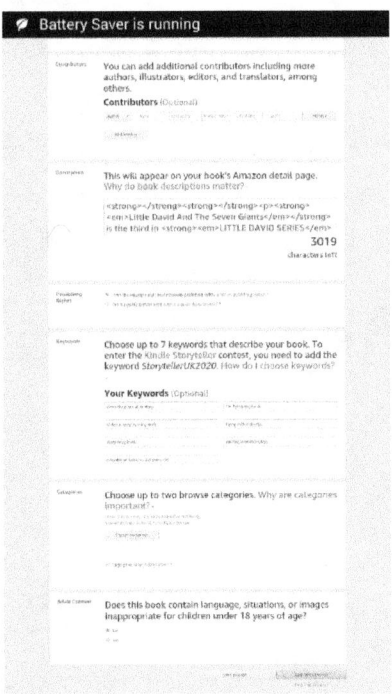

ZERO CAPITAL SELF PUBLISHING SECRETS.

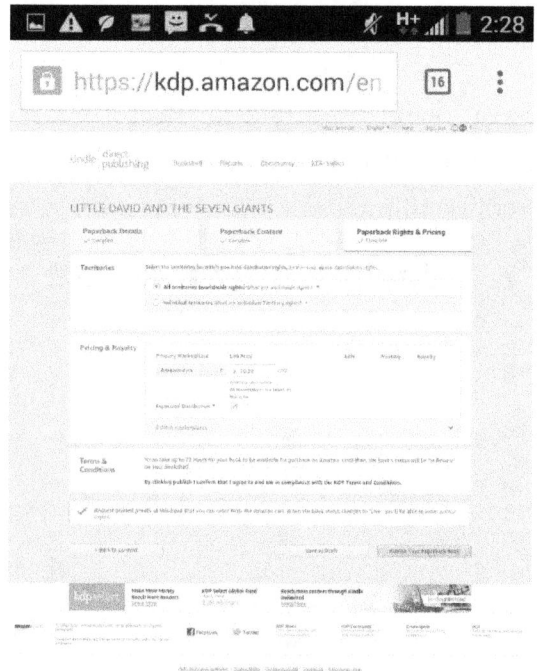

ZERO CAPITAL SELF PUBLISHING SECRETS.

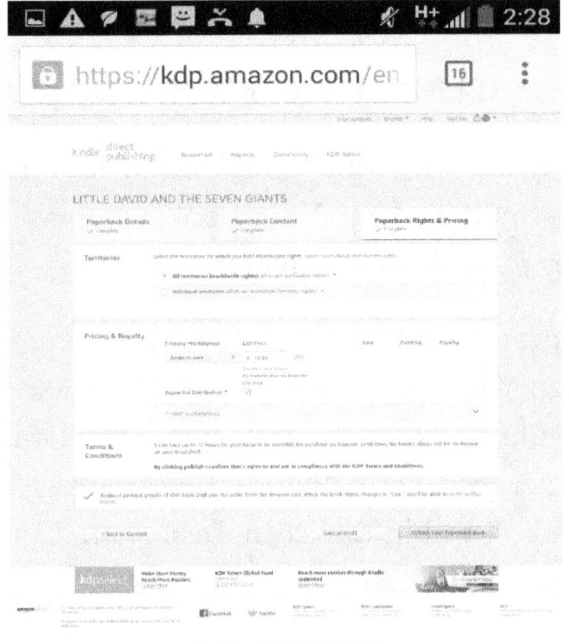

MARKETING YOUR BOOKS.

Writing a book is one thing, making it available to the readers is another thing. Your book will not sell itself; it is your duty to get it to your target audience.

To promote your books, social media is a great place to do that. You should Sign up with them and keep on posting your books and messages. You will make sales. Use Twitter, Facebook, Pinterest, Wordpress, Flipboard, Goodreads, Tumblr, LinkedIn, Instagram, YouTube, and Blogging.

Advertisement is a very effective means to market your books. There are various platforms you can advertise your books by paying their fees. These include Google Adwords, Facebook Ads, Instagram, LinkedIn Ads etc. Also, take advantage of promotional platforms at Amazon, Smashwords, etc.

Download the Smashwords Book Marketing Guide at http://www.smashwords.com/books/view/305

THIRTEEN OTHER WAYS YOU CAN MARKET YOUR BOOKS.

1. Join an online writing community.

2. Join book clubs.

3. Host an online book launch.

4. Host a webinar on your writings.

5. Partner or network with co-authors or writers.

6. Create a website.

7. Start a blog.

8. Start an email newsletter.

9. Start an affiliate programme.

10. Involve in sending out press releases.

11. Get listed in book directories like Goodreads, authorsden, selfpublishersshowcase, bestindiebooks, etc

12. Create a YouTube video about your book.

13. Encourage readers to give honest reviews.

OTHER PLATFORMS TO PUBLISH YOUR BOOKS OR EBOOKS.

This include: Selar, Okadabooks, etc

HOW TO PUBLISH ON SELAR

1. Sign up and set up your bank details

Signing up on Selar is easy and hassle-free. As soon as you sign up, you will be asked to set up and verify your bank details.

2. Upload your products

You can easily upload your books or eBooks on Selar, set your pricing in different currencies, input your books details and customize your books or eBooks links to what you want.

3. Share the link with your customers to pay

Share the link to your store or your product and start receiving payment instantly.

4. Benefits you derive from publishing with Selar

Selar enables Africans sell their digital contents online in multi-currency (NGN, GHS, KES, USD & GBP), while remitting the profit to their bank accounts.

They also connect you to so many affiliates to enable much sales of your products.

HOW TO PUBLISH ON OKADABOOKS

OkadaBooks is a Nigeria online bookstore. To publish on Okadabooks is free and Authors are paid for their books. Okadabooks retain 30% commission. While the authors retain 70%. The author also reserves the right to the book, including the eCopy. The author is at liberty to place any price on his books.

What to do. You can decide to:

1. Create an ePub within OkadaBooks. Or
2. Use Google Docs (For Books without Images apart) Or
3. Use Sigil (Recommended for Comicbooks)

    Watch their video
    https://blog.okadabooks.com/authors/

EXCERPTS.

THE MONKEY WITH SEVEN TAILS.

My mother is a good storyteller. She tells short and interesting stories. She has the knack for describing a scene vividly as if she was there when it happened. Moreover, when making emphasis, she gesticulates by stabbing the air with her fingers in a most pleasant way. We always like her fables, wonder-tales and stories of events that happened long ago when we were not yet born.

On a Monday evening after a busy day's work, my father, mother, brothers and sisters were seated under the shade of the almond tree in front of our compound. It was a hot evening and we were all relaxing with some cold refreshing soft drinks. My mother was having her favourite Goldspot, the fun shine drink. It was now getting dark with the bright moonlight peeping out from behind the clouds on us and we were all ready for another round of storytelling.

"Children, do you know why we have a land tortoise and water turtle? Mother asked picking up her bottle of Goldspot.

"No!" we all chorused. Mother then adjusted herself on her chair and cleared her throat. She sipped from her bottle and looked up. Satisfied that we were anxiously waiting to hear her story, she went on:

A long time ago when animals and men lived together and spoke the same language, there lived Tortoise and his best friend Okoro. They both lived together under one roof and jointly owned a very large farm where they grew food crops like yams, cassava, potatoes and plantains. The time for harvest came.

One day Tortoise sat quietly in his room thinking how rich he would be if he owned the farm alone. He knew that Okoro would never agree. So he thought deeply of various means to remove him out of his way, but he could not find any. This made him very sad.

The next morning, Tortoise came up with a plan and went to the king of the village. He lied to the king that Okoro had boasted before him at home saying, he would do a wonderful thing that would greatly surprise the king and the people in the village. The king was very anxious to hear about the puzzle and immediately, Okoro was summoned to his palace.

It was not long before the news went around the village and a large crowd soon gathered in the palace anxiously waiting to hear what Okoro has got to tell them.

Okoro came into the palace and respectfully prostrated before the king. The king told him that the people in the village were anxiously waiting to learn of the surprise he boasted to Tortoise about.

Okoro was shocked and dumb-founded. He did not see Tortoise the previous day let alone boast of anything. The previous day, he had travelled to the next village to visit his friend, Oriohor who was ill and had spent the night there. How come he had boasted of anything to Tortoise when he had only just arrived? This must be an expensive joke, he thought. The mischievous Tortoise jumped in.

'Okoro, did you not boast to me that you would go to a distant land to bring before the naked eyes of the king, a monkey with seven tails?'

'A monkey with seven tails?' The king asked with his mouth agape.

The crowd burst into an uproar, which kept Okoro dazed for a long time.

'Your lordship, when he thus boasted, I, in turn, boasted that I would lay and hatch hen's eggs to bring out chicks,' said Tortoise hastily as he talked through his nose deceitfully.

Everyone present was surprised. They shouted and cheered excitedly. Some were saying 'wonderful' others were shouting 'unbelievable!' They have never seen a monkey with two tails yet Okoro has boasted of bringing a monkey with seven tails, and as if that was not enough wonder, the sly Tortoise has also boasted to lay and hatch hen's eggs to bring out chicks.

'Wonders shall never end,' a man with pimples all over his face said.

'Maybe the eighth wonder of the world,' a very short man with a big head said to the man with pimples. The king gave Okoro and Tortoise seven days to report to his palace with the fulfilment of their boast or they must surely die. He then ordered them out of his palace.

'I did not, I...' but no one care to listen to Okoro as he tried unsuccessfully to defend himself.

Tortoise swaggered down humming a song: 'Victory! Victory! I have conquered the world! Little did he know that he was making a rod for his own back.

Okoro unhappily walked away still feeling utterly shocked that his best friend could tell such a fatal lie against him. 'Unfaithful friends are no friends', he thought as he walked slowly towards the gate. 'O my God, my God! I am finished!' Okoro cried half-aloud and tried unsuccessfully to belie the tears that rolled down his cheeks as he walked past some women gazing at him by the palace gate.

Thank you for reading my book. If you enjoyed it, won't you please take a moment to leave me a review at your favourite retailer?

Thanks!

David Kprake (Author)

ABOUT DAVID KPRAKE.

David Kprake is an African creative writer of storybooks with good morals, especially for children. He started his writing career in the '80s. The Monkey with Seven Tails is his first published work. His bestselling titles are, Little David series which includes: Little David And His Flying Umbrella; Little David And The Three Angels; & Little David And The Seven Giants. Other of his books Include Ayuwa And The Wicked Queen; The Circumcision; The Tortoise And The Cricket; & Tiny Mosquitoes.

BOOKS BY DAVID KPRAKE.

1. Children storybook. My Father is a Hunter. Kindle Edition
2. The Lost Womb. Children's Storybook. Kindle Edition.
3. Little David And His Flying Umbrella.
4. Little David And The Three Angels
5. Little David And The Seven Giants
6. The Greedy Python.
7. The Tortoise And The Cricket.
8. Tiny Mosquitoes.
9. The Circumcision.
10. The Monkey With Seven Tails.
11. Ayuwa And The Wicked Queen
12. Little David And The Red Dragon With Many Tails.
13. Troubled Minds. The Oracle. (crime series)

Children's Storybook. My Father Is A Hunter. kindle Edition. (Readers series Book 5)

This book is an early learning storybook and reading series with a workbook for children.
Children are result oriented and learn by observation.

This book affords them the opportunity to learn various occupations before they go extinct which includes farming, hunting, fishing etc. They are also made to learn who a doctor is, who a fisherman is and who a hunter is. Here they will learn that 'Garri' is processed from cassava to make a delicious meal. Education is all about learning new things, people, culture, and food.

The Lost Womb. Children's short story.

Kindle Edition

The Lost Womb. Children's short story. Kindle Edition is a thought-provoking story of a travelling gentleman who was faced with a very difficult decision to make between his lovely wife and lovely mother. He is bound to favour one and cause everlasting pain on the other. The question will be a poser to you if you were to face such a dire situation, will you choose your wife against your mother or your mother against your wife. These are tough situations we come across somehow though in different circumstances. Let us know your decision.

Little David And His Flying Umbrella

Little David and his flying umbrella is a wonder story of a little boy who got lost and was to be kidnapped but for the wonderful umbrella in his hand. It is an interesting story for children who love moonlight stories.

Little David and the three Angels

Little David and the three Angels is the second in LITTLE DAVID SERIES. This time, Little David was invited by the police to help in search of the kidnappers who escaped from detention. This series tells of how he was helped by his flying umbrella and angels. The next on the series is, Little David and the seven Giants.

Little David And The Seven Giants

Little David And The Seven Giants is the third in LITTLE DAVID SERIES. This time Little David's village was under attack by some strange giants which made the women unable to trade in the market until Little David was invited to rescue the village. The people have faith in the 'miraculous' power of his flying umbrella.

The Greedy Python.

Mr. Derrick, a friend of one of my father's tenants swayed into my room one morning and met me writing stories. He took my first ever published storybook: the monkey with seven tails, read it and said it was very interesting. He then told me that his family from the United Kingdom are storytellers. Mr Derrick took my pen and drafted three stories. They include The Greedy Python; the proud rabbit & the tortoise; and the three black cats and the fox. One lesson learned from Mr. Derrick that day was that he would always write the morals from every story.

The Tortoise And The Cricket

The Tortoise And The Cricket is a story of greed, lies, tricks and revenge game between the tortoise and the cricket. The one-million-dollar question in this book is, 'who is wiser?' It is an interesting display of wits. At the end, there is just one final winner and a disastrous end of the other. It is a fable loaded with moral lessons for kids. Quite fascinating!

Tiny Mosquitoes

Tiny Mosquitoes is a story for children on how as small as a mosquito is, could make us sick. This book teaches children the value of personal hygiene and how it prevents us from sickness especially in malaria prone cities of Africa.

The Circumcision

The Circumcision is a tortoise story. It is a story of how tortoise craftily posed as a medical doctor in the land of the crickets to revenge an old-time dispute. The crickets were initially doubtful of his integrity but gave in to his cunningness. It is a very interesting fable with lessons to learn. But did tortoise get away with his revenge? Find out! Don't miss to read the series, 'The tortoise and the cricket.'

The Monkey With Seven Tails

The monkey with seven tails is a wonder-tale of a man who wandered into the land of monstrous monkeys due to the false testimony of his friend, the ever mischievous tortoise. The tortoise alleged that Okoro boasted he would bring a monkey with seven tails while tortoise would lay hen's eggs, hatch and produce chicks. No one has seen a monkey with two tails let alone a monkey with seven tails. It is a suspense packed tale of surprises. The next in the series is: "Ayuwa and the wicked Queen". A plot to kill the prince. Truly, the house of the wicked will be destroyed. It is also true that sin and suffering are twins. Read and give a honest review.

Ayuwa And The Wicked Queen

Ayuwa And The Wicked Queen is a folk tale of how a callous tradition almost led to the death of the king-to-be and how his neglected eldest son saved the situation. This feat brought him to limelight which made the wicked queen and her children envious. They plotted to kill the prince but for the God factor or what some call providence. Truly, the house of the wicked will be destroyed. It is also true that sin and suffering are twins.

"The Monkey With Seven Tails" is the first in this series. A tortoise story loaded with surprises. The monkey with seven tails is a wonder-tale of a man who wandered into the land of monstrous monkeys due to the false testimony of his friend, the ever mischievous tortoise. The tortoise alleged that Okoro boasted he would bring a monkey with seven tails while tortoise would lay hen's eggs, hatch and produce chicks. No one has seen a monkey with two tails let alone a monkey with seven tails. It is a suspense-packed tale of surprises.

BOOKS BY DAVID KPRAKE.

Visit Your Favorite Retailers.

OR

TYPE DAVID KPRAKE ON GOOGLE

TYPE DAVID KPRAKE ON AMAZON

ZERO CAPITAL SELF PUBLISHING SECRETS.

NOW OUT TO YOUR FAVOURITE RETAILER

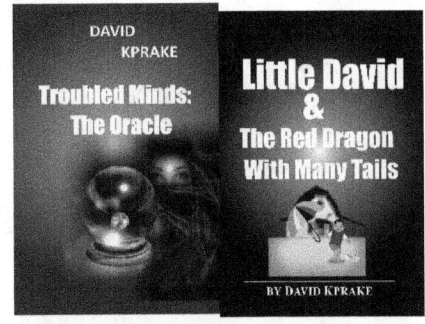

ZERO CAPITAL SELF PUBLISHING SECRETS.

CONNECT DAVID KPRAKE.

Facebook:

https://www.facebook.com/kdtech.boyikprake.5

Twitter:@kprakedave

https://www.amazon.co.uk/David-Kprake/e/B07SHHTT8Z/ref=ntt_dp_epwbk_0

https://www.pinterest.com/kprake/

https://www.goodreads.com/author/show/18805372.David_Kprake

https://www.smashwords.com/books/view/1024221

https://twitter.com/kprakedave/

https://www.instagram.com/newskylight2000/

https://www.facebook.com/kdtech.boyikprake.5

https://www.draft2digital.com/book/495048

https://payhip.com/b/T2Uk

https://payhip.com/b/nmG7

https://payhip.com/b/f4QR

www.ingramcontent.com/pod-product-compliance
Lightning Source LLC
Chambersburg PA
CBHW050310220526
45465CB00005B/1930